Analyzing Labor Education in the 12 Prophets of the Bible

The Education of Labor in the Bible

Bible Sermons

Published by Seminit Publications, 2023.

Table of Contents

Dedication

Isaiah 14:3. *And it shall come to pass in the day that the LORD shall give thee rest from thy sorrow, and from thy fear, and from the hard bondage wherein thou wast made to serve, that thou shalt take up this proverb against the king of Babylon, and say, How hath the oppressor ceased! the golden city ceased!*

O child of God, thou shalt by-and-by have a glorious season of rest! Today is thy time of labour; thou art now under hard bondage; but thou shalt yet come forth into the fullness of thy liberty in Christ Jesus. In that day, Jehovah himself shall give thee rest from all thy grief' and fears; thou shalt obtain joy and gladness, and sorrow and sighing shall flee away. This was a great prophecy for Isaiah to utter, for, in his day, there was no power on earth equal to that of Babylon. That great city abounded in palaces and extraordinary wealth, and its power was such that no kingdom could stand against it. For a while, it broke in pieces all those who fought against it; yet God broke Babylon in his own time; and here is a song of rejoicing in anticipation of its overthrow, «How hath the oppressor ceased! the golden city ceased!»

— **Charles Spurgeon**

General Introduction to the 12 Prophets of the Bible

The books of the Twelve Prophets deal with different circumstances of Israel's life that present different challenges. The unifying theme of these prophets' accounts is that in God there is no separation between the work of worship and the work of daily life, nor between individual well-being and the common good. The people of Israel are faithful or unfaithful to the covenant with God, and the measure of their faithfulness is immediately evident in their worship or neglect of worship. The people's faithfulness or unfaithfulness to the covenant with God is reflected not only in the spiritual realm, but also in the social and physical environment, including the land itself. The degree of the people's faithfulness is also reflected in their life and work ethic, which in turn determines the fruitfulness of their labors and their consequent prosperity or poverty. The wicked may prosper in the short term, but both God's discipline and the natural consequences of unrighteous labor will eventually leave the unrighteous in poverty and desolation. However, when individuals and societies work in faithfulness to God, He blesses them with spiritual, ethical, and environmental health and prosperity.

These last twelve books of the Old Testament are known in the Christian tradition as the Minor Prophets. In the Hebrew tradition, these books are found in a single scroll called "*The Book of Twelve*", which forms a kind of anthology with a progression of thought and thematic coherence. The main background of the collection is the covenant that God has made with his people, and the narrative within the collection is the story of Israel's violation of the covenant and the restoration that God is slowly unfolding for the Israelite nation and society.

In this context, five of the first six books of the Twelve-Joel, Amos, Obadiah, and Micah-reflect the impact of the people's sin, both on the covenant and on world events. The next three - Nahum, Habakkuk, and Zephaniah - speak of the punishment for sin, again in terms of the covenant and the world. The last three prophetic books - Haggai, Zechariah and Malachi - deal with the restoration of Israel, again in terms of a renewal of the covenant and a partial restoration of Israel's position in the world. Finally, Jonah is a special case. His prophecy does not refer to Israel at all, but to the non-Hebrew city-state of Nineveh. It is well known that both its context and its composition are difficult to date reliably.

Who Were the Prophets?

A prophet was one who, called by God and filled with His Spirit, proclaimed the Word of the Lord to people who, in one way or another, had drifted away from God. In a sense, a prophet is a preacher. However, in today's working terms, a prophet is a denouncer, especially when an entire tribe or nation has turned away from God.

Prophets fill the pages of Israel's history. Moses was the prophet God used to rescue the Hebrew people from slavery in Egypt and then to lead them into the land God had promised them. Time and again, this people turned away from God. Moses was God's first spokesman to bring them back into relationship with the Lord. In the Old Testament history books *(Joshua, Judges, 1 and 2 Samuel, 1 and 2 Kings, 1 and 2 Chronicles, Ezra and Nehemiah)*, prophets such as Deborah, Samuel, Nathan, Elijah, Elisha, Huldah and others rise up to speak the Word of God to a rebellious people.

Israel's religious worship was organized around the work of the priests, first in the tabernacle and then in the temple. The description of the daily work of the priests is the slaughtering, butchering, and roasting of the sacrificial animals brought by the people who offered them. However, a priest's job went beyond the hard physical labor of caring for thousands of animal sacrifices. A priest was also responsible for being the spiritual and moral leader of the people. Although the priest was often seen as the mediator between the people and God in the temple sacrifices, his greatest responsibility was to teach the people the law of God (Lev. **10:11**; Deut. **17:8-10**; **33:10**; Ezek. **7:10**).

Unfortunately, it was common in Israel's history for the priests themselves to become corrupt and turn away from God, leading the people into idolatry. The prophets rose up when the priests failed in their task of ruling the land with justice. In a sense, God called the prophets and spoke through them, using them as whistleblowers when the entire Israelite nation was on the verge of self-destruction.

One of the most shocking misfortunes of God's people was that they continually worshiped many of the gods of neighboring pagan nations. Common practices of this idolatrous worship included sacrificing their children to Molech and ritual prostitution with every obscene practice imaginable "*in the high places, on the mountains, and under every green tree*" (**2**Ch **28:4**). But an even greater perversity in abandoning *Yahweh* came from forgetting God's structure for community life as a holy people set apart for God. Care for the poor, the widow, the orphan, and the alien in the land was replaced by oppression. Business practices broke God's standards so that extortion, bribery, and dishonesty became commonplace. Leaders used power to destroy lives, and religious leaders despised what was holy to God. Far from enriching the nation, these ungodly practices brought it to ruin. Typically, prophets were the last voices in the land calling people to return to God and restore their community to health and righteousness.

In most cases, the prophets were not "*professionals*", meaning that they did not make a living from their prophetic activities. God used them for a special task while they were in the midst of their other occupations. Some prophets (such as Jeremiah and Ezekiel) were priests and had the duties described above. Others were shepherds, such as Moses and Amos. Deborah was a judge who settled disputes among the Israelites. Huldah was probably a teacher in the academic sector of Jerusalem. Being a prophet meant having to work.

Locating the prophets within the history of Israel

The records of the earliest prophets are woven into the history of Israel in the books of Joshua through 2 Kings, i.e., they are not found in a separate text. Subsequently, the words and deeds of the prophets were preserved in separate collections that make up the last seventeen books of the Old Testament, from Isaiah to Malachi. These are usually called the *"later prophets"*, or sometimes the *"literary prophets"*, because their words were written in separate literary texts rather than throughout the books of history, as was the case with the earlier prophets.

When the united kingdom split in two, the ten northern tribes (Israel) immediately plunged into idolatry. Elijah and Elisha, the last of the earlier prophets, were called by God to exhort the idolatrous Israelites to worship *Yahweh* alone. The first of the literary prophets, Amos and Hosea, were called to admonish the apostate kings of northern Israel, from Jeroboam II to Hosea. Because both the kings and the people refused to return to *Yahweh*, God allowed the mighty empire of Assyria to overthrow the northern kingdom of Israel in **722** B.C. The Assyrians, cruel and merciless, not only destroyed the cities and towns of the land and plundered their wealth, but also took captives from among the Israelites and scattered them throughout the empire with the intention of destroying their sense of nationhood forever (**2Ki 17:1-23**).

As Israel neared destruction, the small nation of Judah to the south stopped worshipping *Yahweh* and began to worship foreign gods. The good kings made the people give up worship and bad business practices, but the bad kings overruled these actions. In the southern kingdom (Judah), the first literary prophets were Obadiah and Joel, who acted as denouncers during the reigns of Jeroboam, Ahaziah, Joash, and Queen Athaliah.

Isaiah spoke the Word of God in Judah during the reigns of four kings-Uziah, Jotham, Ahaz, and Hezekiah-and Micah also prophesied during this period. Hezekiah's successor on the throne was Manasseh, of whom the Scriptures say that he did more wickedness before the Lord than any of his predecessors (2Ki **21:2-16**).

The accounts of the early prophets are woven into the history of Israel in the books of Joshua through **2** Kings, i.e., they are not found in a separate text. Subsequently, the words and deeds of the prophets were preserved in separate collections that make up the last seventeen books of the Old Testament, from Isaiah to Malachi. These are often called the "*later prophets*", or sometimes the "*literary prophets*", because their words were written in separate literary texts rather than throughout the books of history, as was the case with the earlier prophets.

When the united kingdom split in two, the ten northern tribes (Israel) immediately fell into idolatry. Elijah and Elisha, the last of the earlier prophets, were called by God to exhort the idolatrous Israelites to worship *Yahweh* alone. The first literary prophets, Amos and Hosea, were called to admonish the apostate kings of northern Israel, from Jeroboam II to Hosea. Because both the kings and the people refused to return to *Yahweh*, God allowed the mighty empire of Assyria to overthrow the northern kingdom of Israel in **722** BCE. The cruel and ruthless Assyrians not only destroyed the cities and towns of the land and plundered its wealth, but they also took captives from among the Israelites and scattered them throughout the empire with the intention of destroying their sense of nationhood forever (**2 Kgs 17:1-23**).

As Israel neared destruction, the small southern nation of Judah ceased to worship *Yahweh* and began to worship foreign gods. The good kings caused the people to abandon worship and bad business practices, but the bad kings reversed these actions. In the southern kingdom (Judah), the first literary prophets were Obadiah and Joel, who served as denouncers during the reigns of Jeroboam, Ahaziah, Joash, and Queen Athaliah.

Isaiah proclaimed the Word of God in Judah during the reigns of four kings-Uziah, Jotham, Ahaz, and Hezekiah-and Micah also prophesied during this period. Hezekiah's successor on the throne was Manasseh, who, according to Scripture, did more wickedness before the Lord than any of his predecessors (**2 Ki. 21:2-16**).

Chronology of the biblical prophets

The table below shows where the prophets fit chronologically in the northern kingdom of Israel and the southern kingdom of Judah.

Period	Northern Kings	Northern Prophets	Southern Kings	Southern Prophets
United kingdom under Saul, David, Solomon, c. **1030 - 931**				
Divided kingdom	Jeroboam (**931-910**)		Rehoboam (**931-913**)	
	Nadab (**910-909**)		Abijah (**913**)	
	Baasha (**909-886**)		Asa (**911-870**)	
	Elah (**886**)		Jehoshaphat (**873-848**)	
	Zimri (**885**)		Jehoram (**853-841**)	Obadiah
	Omri (**885-874**)	Elijah	Queen Athaliah (**841-835**)	Joel
		Elisha		Isaiah
	Ahab (**874-853**)	Amos	Joash (**835-796**)	Micah
		Jonah		Jeremiah
	Jehoram (**852-841**)	Hosea	Amaziah (**796-767**)	Zephaniah
				Huldah
	Jehu (**841-814**)		Uzziah (**790-740**)	Nahum
	Jehoahaz (**814-798**)		Jotham (**750-731**)	Habakkuk
	Jehoash (**798-782**)		Ahaz (**735-715**)	
	Jeroboam II (**793-753**)		Hezekiah (**715-686**)	

Zechariah
(**753-752**)
Shallum
(**752**)
Menahem
752-742)
Pekahiah
(**742-740**)
Pekah
(**752-732**)
Hoshea
(**732-722**)

Manasseh
(**695-642**)
Amon
(**642-640**)
Josiah
(**640-609**)
Jehoahaz
(**609**)
Jehoiakim
(**609-597**)
Jehoiachin
(**597**)
Zedekiah
(**597-586**)

Babylonian
exile

Ezekiel
Daniel

Post-exilic
prophets

Zerubbabel,
governor
Nehemiah,
govern

History behind the Twelve Prophets

The context and date of the records of the prophets of Israel and Judah are the subject of much debate.

With respect to the Twelve, we will give a brief description. Within the first group, there is a broad consensus that Hosea, Amos, and Micah date from the eighth century B.C. By this time, the United Kingdom of Israel, ruled by David and later by Solomon, had long since been divided into a northern kingdom known as Israel and a southern kingdom known as Judah. Micah was from the southern kingdom and spoke to the people of his own kingdom, Amos was from the southern kingdom and spoke to the northern kingdom, and Hosea was from the northern kingdom and spoke to the people of his own kingdom.

By the early eighth century, both the northern and southern kingdoms enjoyed prosperity and border security unprecedented since the time of Solomon. But those who had eyes to see, like our prophets, saw that the picture was darkening. Internally, the economic and political situation became more precarious as dynastic strife plagued the ruling class. Externally, the reemergence of Assyria as a superpower in the region posed a growing threat to both kingdoms. In fact, the Assyrian army completely destroyed the northern kingdom around **721** B.C., and it never reemerged as a political entity, although traces of its existence can be found in the Samaritan identity (2Ki **17:1-18**). The prophets rightly blame the people of Israel, and to a lesser extent Judah, for failing to worship *Yahweh* in favor of idolatry and for violating the ethical requirements of the law. Despite these failures, the people were lulled into a false sense of security because of their covenant with *Yahweh* to be His people.

The south, under the rule of King Hezekiah, somewhat survived the Assyrian threat (**2Ki 19**), but faced an even greater challenge with the rise of the Babylonian empire (**2Ki 24**). Unfortunately, Judah did not repent of its idolatry and ethical failings after narrowly escaping the Assyrians. The final defeat came at the hands of the Babylonians in **587** B.C., resulting in the destruction of Judah's social infrastructure and the deportation of its leaders into exile in the Babylonian empire (**2Ki 24-25**). The prophets saw this defeat as evidence of God's punishment of the people. Among the Twelve Prophets, this is most clearly recorded in the books of Nahum, Habakkuk, and Zephaniah. They reflect the prophetic writings of Jeremiah and Ezekiel, which also date from this period. Books other than the Bible record their prophetic careers (*see "Jeremiah and Lamentations and the Work" and "Ezekiel and the Work"*), but we will not discuss them here.

Cyrus, the great Persian king, defeated Babylon and took over its hegemony. In accordance with Persian policy, the empire allowed the Jews to return to their land and, perhaps more importantly, to rebuild their temple and other important institutions (Ez **1**). All of this, it seems, happened because of the will of the Persian Empire. The prophets Haggai, Zechariah and Malachi did their work during this phase of Israel's history.

In summary, the books of the Twelve Prophets cover a wide range of contextual circumstances in the life of the people of God, and therefore show different paradigmatic cases in which it is necessary for faith to be manifested in the work.

The Faith and Work Before Exile - Oseas, Amos, Obadiah, Joel and Micah

Hosea, Amos, Obadiah, Joel, and Micah served as prophets in the eighth century B.C., when the state was well developed but the economy was in decline. Power and wealth were accumulating in the upper classes, leaving one social class at a disadvantage. There is evidence that farmers began to focus on cash crops that could be sold to the growing urban population. This had the destabilizing effect of leaving peasants with a combination of crops and animals that could not withstand the loss of any one crop or market. Peasant communities became vulnerable to annual fluctuations in production, and as a result, cities were exposed to ups and downs in their food supply (Am **4:6-9**). By the time the prophets of this era began to speak, the glory days of opulent building projects and territorial expansion were long gone. Such circumstances were a breeding ground for corruption by those desperate to cling to their declining power and wealth, and for a widening gap between the rich and the poor. As a result, God's prophets of this period have much to contribute to the world of work.

God Requires a Transformation (Hosea 1:1-9; Micah 2:1-5)

God blames the people as a whole for the corruption of Israel. They have abandoned the covenant with God, which breaks both their relationship with God and the righteous social structures of the Lord's law, and leads directly to corruption and economic decline. The term the prophets often use to describe Israel's covenant violation is "*harlotry*" (e.g., Jer **3:2**; Ezek **23:7**). To dramatize the situation, God takes the metaphor literally and commands the prophet Hosea, "*Take a harlot for yourself and beget children of whoredom; for the land has grievously played the harlot and has forsaken the LORD*" (Hos **1:2**). Hosea obeys God's command and marries a woman named Gomer, who apparently fulfills the requirement, and has three children by her (Hos **1:3**). This leaves us to imagine what it must have been like to make a home and raise children with a harlot.

Although the prophets use the imagery of prostitution and adultery, God accuses Israel of economic and social corruption, not sexual immorality.

Woe to those who plan iniquity, who plot evil in their beds! In the morning light they carry it out, for it is in the power of their hands. They covet fields and seize them, houses and take them. They rob the owner and his house, the man and his inheritance (Mic **2:1-2**).

This makes the situation of Hosea's family a dramatic example for those working in corrupt or imperfect places today. God intentionally placed Hosea in a corrupt and difficult family situation. Is it possible for God to deliberately place people in corrupt and difficult workplaces today? While it is possible to seek a comfortable job with a reputable employer in a respectable profession, we may be able to accomplish much more for the kingdom of God by working in places that have made moral compromises. If you abhor corruption, can you fight it more effectively by working as a lawyer in a prestigious firm or as a building inspector in a mafia-ridden city? There are no easy answers, but God's call to Hosea suggests that making a difference in the world is more important to God than staying away from sin. As Dietrich Bonhoeffer wrote in the midst of Nazi-controlled Germany, "*The most important question a responsible man must ask himself is not how to get out of the situation heroically, but how the next generation will live*".

Dios permite el cambio (Oseas 14:1-9; Amós 9:11-15; Miqueas 4:1-5; Abdías 21)

The same God who demands change also promises to make change possible. "*A harvest is prepared, when I will restore the welfare of my people. When I will heal Israel*" (Hos **6:11-7:1**). The Twelve Prophets convey a crucial optimism that God is at work in the world to change it for the better. Despite the apparent triumph of evil, God is ultimately in charge and "*the kingdom will be the Lord's*" (Obad **21**). In spite of the misfortunes people bring upon themselves, God is at work to restore the goodness with which life and work were designed from the beginning. He is "*compassionate and gracious, slow to anger and abounding in love*" (Joel **2:13**). The final prophecies of Joel, Hosea and Amos illustrate this in explicit economic terms.

The threshing floors will be full of grain, and the jars will overflow with new wine and new oil... You shall eat your fill and be satisfied; and you shall praise the name of the LORD your God, who has dealt marvelously with you; and my people shall never be ashamed. (Joel **2:24, 26**)

[The Israelites who dwell in His shadow shall again grow wheat and flourish like the vine. Their glory will be like the wine of Lebanon (Hos **14:7**).

I will restore the prosperity of My people Israel, and they shall rebuild the desolate cities and dwell in them; they shall also plant vineyards and drink their wine, and they shall cultivate gardens and eat their fruit. (Am **9:14**)

God's word to His people in times of economic and social hardship is that He intends to restore peace, justice, and prosperity if the people will live according to the precepts of His covenant. The means God chooses to use is the work of His people.

Unjust Labour: A Study of Miqueas 1:1-7; 3:1-2

———

Despite God's intentions, work is subject to human sin. The most obvious case is work that is inherently sinful. Micah mentions prostitution, in this case probably that which took place in sacred rituals, and promises that the proceeds will be burned with fire (Mic 1:7). A simple application would be to exclude prostitution from legitimate occupations, even though it may be an understandable choice for those who have no other way to support themselves and their families. There are other works that also raise the question of whether or not they should be performed. We can all think of various examples, no doubt, and Christians would do well to seek work that benefits others and society as a whole.

But Micah is speaking to Israel as a whole, not just individually. He is criticizing a society in which social, economic, and religious conditions make prostitution a viable option. The question is not whether it is acceptable to earn a living through prostitution, but how society must change so that no one feels the need to engage in degrading or harmful work. Micah calls for leaders who do not reform society to be held accountable, not those who are forced into harmful work. His words are harsh. *"Hear now, O heads of Jacob and rulers of the house of Israel: is it not for you to know righteousness? You who hate the good and love the evil, who tear off their skin and their flesh from their bones"* (Mic 3:1-2).

There are both similarities and differences between Micah's society and ours. The specific solutions God promises to the ancient people of Israel are not necessarily what God intends for our time. Micah's prophetic words reflect the relationship between prostitution in sacred rites and idolatrous cults in his day. God promises to put an end to the social ills concentrated in sectarian sanctuaries. *"I will eradicate your carved images and your sacred pillars from your midst, and you will no longer bow down to the work of your hands. I will uproot your Asherahs from among you, and I will destroy your cities"* (Mic **5:13-14**). In our day, we need God's wisdom to find effective solutions to the current social factors that encourage sinful and oppressive work.

Working Unjustly (Hosea 4:1-10; Amos 5:10-15; 8:5-6; Joel 2:28-29)

When the prophets speak of fornication, they almost never refer only to this particular type of work. Often they also use it as a metaphor for unrighteousness, which by its very nature is unfaithfulness to God's covenant (Hos **4:7-10**). With a general reminder that wages can be earned unfairly, Amos indicts merchants who use substandard products, false weights, and other deceptions to make a profit at the expense of vulnerable consumers. He makes several specific charges against Israelite labor practices because labor in Israel has become unfair and oppressive (Am **5:7**). There, those who speak out against corruption and exploitation - or even those who simply speak the truth - are silenced (Am **5:10**). Businessmen use their power to exploit the poor and the weak (Am **5:11**). The law is no obstacle to their exploitation because there are many officials who are willing to take bribes to ignore the situation. In fact, the government has completely abdicated its responsibility to care for the poor (Am **5:12**). In all of these cases, the problem is not that the Israelites have jobs that are inherently evil; the problem is that they misrepresent the offices that God wants them to use for good-business, real estate, law, and government-by turning them into forms of oppression. They wonder when it is time to *"shorten the ephah, and increase the shekel [cheat on the measures], and deceive with false balances; to buy the poor and needy for the* *price of a pair of sandals, and to sell the refuse of the wheat*" (Am **8:5-6**).

Many of today's professions, by which people earn a legitimate living, can become unjust in the way they are practiced. Should a photographer take pictures of anything a client asks for without considering the effect on himself and others who will see the result? Should a surgeon perform any kind of elective surgery for which a patient is willing to pay? Is a mortgage broker responsible for ensuring that a potential borrower has the ability to repay the loan without undue hardship? Is it right not to help colleagues who are failing because their failure makes us look better by comparison? If our work is a form of service to God, we cannot ignore such questions. However, we must be careful not to believe that there is a hierarchy of ministries. The claim of the prophets is not that some kinds of work are more godly than others, but that all kinds of work should be done as a contribution to God's work in the world. God promises that "*in those days I will pour out my Spirit on the menservants and on the maidservants*" (Joel **2:29**).

La Interdependencia de los Individuos y las Comunidades (Amós 8:1-6; Miqueas 6:1-16)

Fairness in the workplace is not just an individual issue. Individuals have a responsibility to ensure that everyone in society has access to the resources necessary to make a living. The clearest way Amos criticizes Israel for injustice in this regard is through an allusion to the law of gleaning. Gleaning is the process of gathering the leftover grain in a field after the harvesters have passed. According to the covenant between God and Israel, farmers were not allowed to glean in their own fields, but were to allow the poor (literally, *"widows and orphans"*) to glean in their fields for their sustenance (Deut. **24:19**). This created a rudimentary form of social welfare based on giving the poor the opportunity to work (glean) so that they would not have to beg, steal, or starve. Gleaning is a way to participate in the dignity of work, even for those who are unable to participate in the labor market due to lack of resources, socioeconomic disruption, discrimination, disability, or other factors. God not only wants everyone's needs to be met, but also wants everyone to have the dignity of working to meet their needs and the needs of others.

Amos complains that this commandment is being violated. The farmers do not leave the leftover grain in their fields for the poor to gather (Mic **7:1-2**). Instead, they choose to sell the chaff-the refuse left over after threshing-to the poor at an exorbitant price.

"*Hear this, you who trample on the needy and would destroy the poor of the land*", Amos accuses them of selling "*the refuse of the wheat*" (Am **8:4, 6**), and he reproaches them for looking forward to the end of the Sabbath so that they can continue to sell this cheap, adulterated edible product to those who have no other choice (Am **8:5**).

Furthermore, they cheat even those who can afford pure grain, as evidenced by the fraudulent scales in the marketplace. They boast, We will make the ephah [the wheat for sale] smaller and the shekel [the price for sale] larger. Micah proclaims God's judgment against unjust trade. "*Can I justify false scales and deceitful bags of weights?*" says the Lord (Mic **6:11**). This tells us clearly that justice is not only a matter of criminal law and political expression, but also of economic opportunity. The ability to work to meet individual and family needs is essential to the role of the individual in the covenant. Economic justice is a fundamental component of Micah's famous and resonant statement just three verses earlier: "*And what does the LORD require of you but to do justice and to love mercy and to walk humbly with your God*" (Micah **6:8**). God requires of His people, as a daily aspect of their walk with Him, to love mercy and to do justice, individually and socially, in all aspects of work and economic life.

Work and Devotion (Micah 6:6-8; Amos 5:21-24; Hosea 4-11)

In the eyes of the prophet, justice is not simply a secular matter. Micah's call for justice in verse **6:8** follows the observation that justice is better than extravagant religious sacrifices (Mic **6:6-7**). Hosea and Amos develop this point. Through Amos, God opposes the separation of religious fulfillment from ethical action.

I abhor and despise your feasts, nor do I delight in your solemn assemblies. Though you offer me burnt offerings and your grain offerings, I will not accept them, nor will I consider the peace offerings of your fattened animals. Take away from me the noise of your songs, for I will not even listen to the music of your harps. But let justice roll down like waters, and righteousness like an ever-flowing stream (Am **5:21-24**).

Hosea shows us more deeply the relationship between being spiritually grounded and doing good work. Good work flows directly from faithfulness to God's covenant, and conversely, bad work leads us away from God's presence.

Hear the word of the LORD, O children of Israel, for the LORD has a controversy with the inhabitants of the land, because there is no faithfulness, no mercy, and no knowledge of God in the land. There is only perjury, lying, murder, robbery, and adultery. They use violence, and murder follows murder. Therefore the earth mourns, and every one who dwells in it languishes, along with the beasts of the field and the birds of the sky; even the fish of the sea perish... My people are destroyed for lack of knowledge. Because you have rejected knowledge, I will also reject you, so that you will not be my priest; because you have forgotten the law of your God, I will also forget your children. (Hos **4:1-3, 6**)

In truth, if we refuse to do righteous, ethical, and good work, it calls into question our claim to be worshipers of God. If we set aside one day a week to worship God, but then ignore His ways the other six days, does that one day of worship represent who we really are? Hosea complains that the wickedness of Israel's work belies their worship of God. Their work is fraudulent, exemplified by the border guards who move to cheat their neighbors out of part of their land (Hos **5:10**). They practice deception (Hos **7:1**), even as they profess to worship the Lord (Hos **8:13-14**) and fail to keep their promises (Hos **10:4**). To validate their evil ways, they form political alliances with oppressive foreign powers (Hos **11:5-12:1**). They misuse their God-given ability to work (Hos **13:2**). They appear religious but do not obey God (Hos **11:7**). Their corruption and injustice in the workplace are actually signs that they have become devoted to false gods (Hos **9:7-17**).

This is a reminder that the world of work is not separate from the rest of life. If we do not work according to God's covenant values and priorities, our lives and work will be ethically and spiritually inconsistent. How we work during the week is not so much a question of whether we are obedient to the God we worship, but whether we actually worship God. If God is not the God of our lives every day, then it is likely that He is not really our God on

Sunday. If we do not please God in our work, we cannot please Him in our worship.

Apathy Due to Wealth (Amos 3:9-15; 6:1-7)

The prophets criticize those whose wealth leads them to abandon work for the common good and those who abandon any sense of responsibility for their neighbor. Amos links idle wealth to oppression when he accuses the idle rich of doing evil, being violent, and stealing (Am **3:10**). God will quickly put an end to the wealth of such people. He says, "*I will also overthrow the winter house with the summer house; the ivory houses will also perish*" (Am **3:15**). Amos launches a blast of severe criticism against the luxury of "*those who dwell at ease in Zion*" (Am **6:1**), pointing out that they live quietly as they "*lie on their beds*" (Am **6:4**) and "*improvise to the sound of the harp*" (Am **6:5**). When God punishes Israel, "*they will now go into exile at the head of the exiles*" (Am **6:7**).

Today we hear strikingly similar complaints against those who have wealth but do not use it for good. This applies to individuals as well as to corporations, governments and other institutions that use their wealth to exploit the vulnerability of others rather than to create something useful commensurate with their wealth. Many Christians - perhaps most in the West - have some capacity to change these things, at least in their immediate working environment. The words of the prophets are an ongoing challenge and encouragement to care deeply about how our work and wealth serve - or do not serve - the needs of those around us.

The Faith and Labour of Nahum, Habakkuk and Zephaniah Whilst in Exile

Nahum, Habakkuk, and Zephaniah prophesied at a time when the southern kingdom was in rapid decline. Internal dissension and external pressure from the prosperous Babylonian Empire caused Judah to become a vassal state of Babylon. Shortly thereafter, in **587** B.C., a foolish rebellion brought the wrath of the Babylonians upon them, resulting in the collapse of the state of Judah and the deportation of the elite to the heart of the Babylonian empire (2Ki **24-25**). In exile, the people of Israel had to find a way to be faithful even though they were separated from their major religious institutions such as the temple, the priesthood, and even the land. If, as we have seen, the first six books deal with the effects of the people's sin, Nahum, Habakkuk and Zephaniah refer to the punishment that resulted from sin during this period.

God's Punishment in the Workplace (Nahum 1:1-12; Habakkuk 3:1-19; Zephaniah 1:1-13)

Nahum's main contribution is to clarify that the political and economic disaster is God's punishment or discipline for Israel. God declares that He has afflicted them (Nah **1:12**). Habakkuk and Zephaniah explain that an important part of God's punishment is the people's diminished ability to earn a satisfactory living.

The fig tree will not bud, nor will there be any fruit in the vineyards; the olive tree will not yield its fruit, nor will the fields yield their crops; the flock will not come forth from the fold, nor will there be any herd in the stalls (Hab **3:17**).

All the people of Canaan shall be silenced, and all who weigh silver shall be cut off (Zeph **1:11**).

So, are today's political, economic, and natural disasters a punishment from God? There are many people who are willing to claim that certain disasters are signs of God's wrath. The governor of Tokyo and an MSNBC news anchor attributed the **2011** earthquake and tsunami in Japan to divine punishment. But unless we join the ranks of the Twelve or the other prophets of Israel, we should not glibly declare that God's wrath is manifested in world events. Was it God Himself who revealed the reasons for the tsunami to these commentators, or did they draw their own conclusions? Did He reveal His purpose to a considerable number of people well in advance, over many years, as He did to the prophets of Israel, or did it come to one or two people the next day? Were those who proclaim God's judgment in modern times, like the prophets, brought about by years of suffering along with the afflicted, as was the case with Jeremiah, the Twelve, and the other prophets of the ancient people of Israel?

Idolatrous Labor (Habakkuk 2:1-20; Zephaniah 1:14-18)

The blame for the punishment lies with the people themselves. They have worked unfaithfully, turning good materials of stone, wood, and metal into idols. But the work of making idols is worthless, no matter how costly the materials or how well done the results.

Of what use is the idol that its maker has carved, or the molten image, master of lies, if its maker trusts in his work when he makes dumb idols (Hab. **2:18**).

As Zephaniah puts it, *"Neither their silver nor their gold can deliver them"* (Zeph **1:18**). Faithfulness is not a superficial thing that leads us to worship God while we work. It is the act of making God's priorities our priorities at work. Habakkuk reminds us that *"the LORD is in his holy temple; let all the earth keep silence before him"* (Hab **2:20**). This silence is not just a religious fulfillment, but involves silencing our own ambitions, fears, and evil motivations so that God's covenant priorities can become our priorities. Consider what awaits those who defraud others in banking and finance.

"Woe to him who increases what is not his (for how long?) and becomes rich by borrowing!" Will not your creditors suddenly rise up and your debt collectors awake? Surely you will be a prey to them (Hab **2:6-7**).

Those who hoard their ill-gotten gains in real estate, a phenomenon that seems to be constant throughout the ages, are also snares to themselves.

Woe to him who makes illicit gain for his house, to set his nest on high, to deliver himself from the hand of calamity! You have devised a shameful thing for your house, destroying many peoples, sinning against yourself. Surely the stone shall cry out from the wall, and the beam shall answer him from the frame (Hab **2:9-11**).

People who exploit the vulnerabilities of others also bring judgment upon themselves.

Woe to him who gives his neighbor drink; woe to you who mixes your poison until you intoxicate him, to behold his nakedness! Thou shalt be filled with dishonor rather than with glory. Drink you also and show your nakedness. The cup of the Lord's right hand shall return upon thee, and shame upon thy glory (Hab **2:15-16**).

Work that oppresses or takes advantage of others ultimately causes its own downfall.

Today, we may not be making idols out of precious materials to which we bow, but work can also be idolatrous if we believe we are capable of producing our own salvation. The essence of idolatry *"is trusting in something made by your own hands"* (Hab **2:18**, NTV, compare with NKJV above) instead of trusting in the God who created us to work with His guidance and power. If we covet power and influence because we believe that without our wisdom, skill and leadership our work group, our company, organization or nation is destined for failure, our ambition is a form of idolatry. Conversely, if we desire power and influence to bring others into a network of service in which everyone produces God's gifts to the world, then our ambition is a form of faithfulness. If our response to success is to congratulate ourselves, we are practicing idolatry. If our response is gratitude, we are worshiping God. If our reaction to failure is desolation, we are feeling the emptiness of a broken idol. But if our reaction is faith to try again, we are experiencing the saving power of God.

Fidelity Amidst Toil (Habakkuk 2:1; Zephaniah 2:1-4)

Another dynamic is at work in the exile. Despite the emphasis on punishment in Nahum, Habakkuk, and Zephaniah, people also began to relearn how to work in faithful service to God during this time. This is explored more fully in other chapters, such as *"Jeremiah and Lamentations and Work"* and *"Daniel and Work"*, but it is also implied here in the books of the Twelve. The key point is that even in the harrowing circumstances of exile, it is still possible to be faithful. When Habakkuk saw the carnage around him and no doubt wished he were somewhere else, he chose to stay at his post and listen to God's word (Hab **2:1**). But it is possible to do more than just stay at the post, valuable as that is. We can also find a way to be righteous and humble.

Seek the Lord, all you humble of the earth who have kept His commandments; seek righteousness, seek humility. Perhaps you will be saved in the day of the Lord's wrath (Zeph **2:3**).

There are no ideal workplaces. Some are profoundly difficult for God's people, with compromises in many ways, while others are flawed in more general ways. But even in difficult workplaces, we can be faithful witnesses to God's purposes, both in the quality of our presence and the quality of our work. Habakkuk reminds us that no matter how unfruitful our work may seem, God is there with us, giving us a joy that even the worst working conditions could not completely extinguish.

> *Though the fig tree does not bud,*
>
> *and there is no fruit on the vine;*
>
> *Though the olive tree is not yielding its fruit*
>
> *and the fields yield no food;*
>
> *Though there be no sheep in the sheepfold*
>
> *and the cows are not in their stalls,*
>
> *yet I will rejoice in the Lord,*
>
> *I will rejoice in the God of my salvation.*
>
> *The Lord God is my strength;*
>
> *He has made my feet like the feet of a donkey,*
>
> *He maketh me to walk on high (Hab. **3:17-19**).*

Or, as Terry Barringer paraphrases it,

> *Even though the contract is up,*
>
> *And no jobs are available;*
>
> *Though there is no demand for my skills,*
>
> *And no one publishes my work.*
>
> *Even if the savings run out,*

And the pension is not enough to support me;

I will still rejoice in the Lord,

I will rejoice in the God of my salvation.

As verse **19** points out, good work is possible even in the midst of difficult circumstances because the Lord is our strength. Faithfulness is not just a matter of enduring hardship, but of improving even the worst situation in every way we can.

The Faith and the Labor After Exile - Haggai, Zechariah and Malachi

When the exile ended, Jewish civil and religious life was restored in the land of God's promise. Jerusalem and its temple were rebuilt, along with the economic, social, and religious infrastructure of Jewish society. Consequently, the books of the Twelve now mention the challenges of the work that follows sin and punishment.

The Requirement of Social Capital
(Haggai 1:1-2:19)

O ne of the challenges we face in the workplace is the temptation to put ourselves and our families ahead of the community. The prophet Haggai paints a vivid picture of this challenge. He confronts people who, while working hard to rebuild their own homes, do not contribute resources to the rebuilding of the temple, the center of Jewish society. "*Is it time for you to dwell in your cassette houses while this house is desolate?*" (Hg **1:4**). He says that not investing in social capital actually reduces individual productivity.

You sow much, but reap little; you eat, but there is not enough to satisfy you; you drink, but there is not enough to make you drunk; you clothe yourselves, but no one warms himself; and he who receives wages receives wages in a broken purse. (Hg **1:6**)

But as the Lord awakens the spirit of the people and their leaders, they begin to invest in rebuilding the temple and the fabric of society (Hg **1:14-15**).

Investing in social capital reminds us that there is no such thing as a "*man who has gotten ahead by his own efforts*". While individual effort can accumulate great wealth, each of us depends on resources and social infrastructure that ultimately come from God. "*I will fill this house with glory*", says the Lord of hosts. "*Mine is the silver and mine is the gold*" - declares the Lord of hosts (**2:7-8**). Prosperity is not only - not even primarily - a matter of personal effort, but of a community based on the covenant with God. "*The latter glory of this house will be greater than the former*", says the Lord of hosts (Heb **2:9**).

We are foolish to think that we must provide for ourselves before we can devote time to God and the fellowship of His people. The truth is that we cannot provide for ourselves except by the grace of God's generosity and the mutual labor of His community. This is the same concept behind the tithe. It is not a sacrifice to give ten percent of a harvest, but a blessing of one hundred percent of the amazing productivity of God's creation.

In our day, this reminds us of the importance of investing resources in the material aspects of life. Physical needs such as housing, food, cars, and others are important, but God provides enough in abundance that we can also invest in aspects such as art, music, education, nature, recreation, and the many ways to feed the soul. Like the entrepreneur or the carpenter, those who work in the arts, humanities, or recreation, or who give money to build parks, playgrounds, and theaters, make an equally important contribution to the world God has created.

This also suggests that investing in churches and church life is crucial to strengthening the work of Christians. Worship itself is closely related to doing good work, as we have seen, and perhaps we should engage in worship that shapes good work, not just devotion or private enjoyment. Moreover, the Christian community could be a powerful force for economic, civic, and social good if it learned to bring the spiritual and ethical power of God's Word to bear on issues of work in the economic, social, governmental, academic, and scientific arenas.

The Work, Worship, and Environment: Hageo 1:1-2:19; Zechariah 7:8-14

Haggai makes the connection between the social and economic well-being of the people and the state of the environment. In a play on words that is most evident in the Hebrew language, Haggai relates the desolation of the temple (*"desolate"*, the Hebrew term hareb, Hag **1:9**) to the desolation of the land and its crops (*"drought"*, the Hebrew term horeb) and the resulting ruin of the general welfare of *"men, cattle, and all the work of your hands"* (Hag **1:11**). The key element in this relationship is the condition of the temple, which becomes an indicator of the religious faithfulness or unfaithfulness of the people. There is a threefold relationship between worship, socio-economic health, and the environment. If there is a disease in our physical environment, there is a disease in human society, and one of the signs of the malaise of a society is its contribution to the disease of the environment.

There is also a relationship between the economic and political condition of a community and the way it worships and cares for the earth. The prophets call us to remember that respect for the Creator of the earth on which we live is a starting point for peace between the earth and its inhabitants. For Haggai, there is a connection between the drought of the land and the ruin of the temple. True and sincere worship opens the door to peace and blessing for the land.

From the day the foundation of the Lord's Temple was laid, consider well: "*Is the seed yet in the barn? The vine, the fig tree, the pomegranate tree, and the olive tree have not yet borne fruit; but from this day I will bless you*". (Hg **2:18-19**)

Zechariah also points to a connection between human sin and the desolation of the earth. The powerful oppress the widow, the fatherless, the stranger, and the poor (Zech **7:10**). "*And they hardened their hearts like unto diamonds, that they would not hearken unto the law, nor unto the words which the LORD of hosts sent*" (Zech **7:12**). As a result, the environment was degraded and "*they turned the desirable land into a desolation*" (Zech **7:14**). Joel, however, had observed the beginnings of this degradation long before the exile: "*The vine is withering, the fig tree is withering, the pomegranate tree, the palm tree, the apple tree, all the trees of the field are withering. The joy of the children of men is dried up*" (Joel **1:12**).

Given the importance of work and work practices for the well-being of the environment, Christians could have a profoundly beneficial impact on the planet and all who inhabit it if we worked according to the vision of the Twelve Prophets. Faithful people have an urgent environmental responsibility to learn concrete ways in which they can ground their work in the worship of God.

Haggai's extended prophecy concerning purity (Hag **2:10-19**) also indicates a relationship between purity and the well-being of the earth. God complains that because of the impurity of the people, "*every work of their hands and what they offer here is unclean*" (Hag **2:14**). This is part of the more global relationship between worship and the well-being of the environment. One possible application is that a pure environment is an environment that is treated sustainably by those to whom God has given responsibility for its well-being, i.e., humanity. Thus, purity entails a basic respect for the integrity of the entire created order, the health of its ecosphere, the viability and well-being of its species, and the renewability of its productivity. And so, we return to the issue of Christians and responsible labor practices.

Therefore, if desolation is part of God's punishment for the sin of the people recorded in the book of the Twelve, then productive land is part of restoration. In fact, under quite different circumstances, Zechariah had a vision similar to that of Amos during Israel's time of prosperity, in which the people experience well-being by sitting under the fig trees they had planted. "*In that day*", declares the Lord of hosts, "*you shall invite each one his neighbor under his vine and under his fig tree*" (Zech **3:10**). Peace with God includes caring for the land that God has created. Productive land, of course, must be worked to obtain the fruit, and therefore, the world of work is intimately related to the materialization of abundant life.

Sin and Hope Remain Present in the Work (Malachi 1:1-4:6)

———

Even in the time of restoration, human sin still exists. Malachi, the third of the restoration prophets, complains that some people are beginning to profit by exploiting the most vulnerable in Israelite society, especially by cheating workers out of their wages (Mal **3:5**). God himself tells them that when they defraud others, "*you rob me*" (Mal **3:8**, emphasis added). Not surprisingly, such people also pollute temple worship by saving what they contribute in offerings (Mal **1:8-19**), and the environment is affected as a result (Mal **3:11**).

Nevertheless, the hope of the prophets remains, and at its heart is the work. It begins with the promise to restore the religious and social infrastructure of the temple.

Behold, I am sending My messenger, and he will prepare the way before Me. The Lord whom you seek will come suddenly to His temple, and the messenger of the covenant in whom you delight, behold, he is coming, says the Lord of hosts (Mal **3:1**).

And it continues with the restoration of the environment. God promises, "*I will rebuke the devourer*" (Mal **3:11**a) and adds that it will be "*a land of delight*" (Mal **3:12**). People work with ethical principles (Mal **3:14, 18**), and one result is that the economy is restored, including "*the fruit of the earth*" and "*your vine in the field*" (Mal **3:11**).

Jonah and the Blessing of God for All Nations

As noted in the introduction, the book of Jonah is atypical among the Twelve Prophets because its story does not take place in Israel, the text is not dated and does not contain prophetic predictions, and the focus is not on the people to whom the prophet is sent but on his personal experience. However, Jonah agrees with the other prophets that God is active in the world (Jn **1:2, 17; 2:10**) and that faithfulness (or unfaithfulness) to God maintains a tripartite relationship between worship, socioeconomic health, and the environment. When the sailors pray to the Lord and obey His word, the sea is calmed and God provides what is necessary for the sailors and Jonah to be well (Jn **1:14-17**). When Jonah returns to proper worship, the Lord restores the environment to its proper order: the fish in the sea and the people on dry land (Jon **2:7-10**). When Nineveh chooses to listen to the Lord, animals and humans are united in harmony, and socioeconomic violations cease (Jonah **3:4-10**). Although Jonah's context is different from that of the rest of the Twelve Prophets, his lesson is not. The special contributions of the book of Jonah are (**1**) the focus on the prophet's call and response, and (**2**) the recognition that God's work to bless Israel is not against other nations, but that He desires to bless other nations through Israel.

The Call and Response of Jonah
(Jonah 1:1-17)

Like the Twelve Prophets, the book of Jonah begins with a call from God (Jon **1:1-2**). Unlike the others, however, Jonah rejects this call and foolishly attempts to escape the presence of the Lord by boarding a ship bound for a foreign land (Jon **1:3**). This puts not only himself in danger, but also those on the ship, for as we have seen throughout the book of Twelve, breaking the covenant with God has tangible consequences, and the actions of individuals always affect the community. God sends a storm that first ruins the sailors' business prospects by forcing them to throw all their goods into the sea to lighten the load (Jn **1:5**). And finally, it threatens their own lives (Jn **1:11**). The storm calms and the danger to the community disappears only when Jonah suggests that they throw them into the sea (Jn **1:12-15**), which the sailors reluctantly accept.

The purpose of a call from God is to serve others, and Jonah's call is to benefit Nineveh. When he rejects God's guidance, not only are the people he is called to serve weakened, but those around him suffer as well. When we accept that we are all called to serve God in our work - which may be different from Jonah's, but no less important to God - we recognize that when we fail to do so, we hurt our communities. The greater our gifts and talents, the greater the harm we can do by rejecting God's leading in our work. We certainly know people whose prodigious abilities allow them to do great harm in business, government, society, science, religion, and all the rest. Imagine the good they could have done, the evil they could have avoided, if they had first submitted their abilities to the worship and service of the Lord. Our gifts may seem insignificant in comparison, but imagine the good we could do and the evil we could avoid if we did our work as a lifelong service to God.

God's Blessing to All Nations (Jonah 1:16; 3:1-4:2)

Jonah disobeys God's call because he opposes the Lord's desire to bless Israel's enemies, the nation of Assyria and its capital, Nineveh. When he finally relents and his mission is successful, he is dismayed at God's mercy toward them (Jn **4:1-2**). This is understandable, since Assyria was conquering the northern kingdom of Israel at the time (**2Ki 17:6**), and Jonah was sent to bless the people he detested. But this is God's will. Apparently, God's desire is to use the people of Israel to bless all nations, not just themselves. (See *"Blessing for All Nations"*, Jeremiah **29**, in *"Jeremiah and Lamentations and the Work"*, above).

Is it possible that everyone tries to put their own limits on the scope of God's blessing through their work? We often believe that we should hoard the benefits of our work for ourselves, lest others gain an advantage over us. We may resort to secrecy and deception, cheating and shortcuts, exploitation and intimidation in an effort to get ahead of our rivals in the workplace. We seem to accept as fact the unproven assumption that our success at work must come at the expense of others. Have we convinced ourselves that success is a zero-sum game?

God's blessing is not a bucket of limited capacity, but an overflowing fountain. "*Prove me now*", says the Lord of hosts, "*if I do not open the windows of heaven for you and pour out blessing until it overflows*" (Mal **3:10**). Despite the competition, resource constraints, and malice that we often face in the workplace, God's mission for us is not something as trivial as survival against the odds, but the miraculous transformation of our workplaces to achieve the creativity and productivity, relationships and social harmony, and environmental balance that God planned from the beginning.

Although Jonah initially refuses to participate in God's blessing on his adversaries, his faithfulness to God ultimately overcomes his disobedience. Finally, he decides to warn Nineveh, and to his chagrin, its citizens respond passionately to his message. The whole city, *"from the greatest to the least"* (Jon **3:5**), from the king and his nobles to the people in the streets and the animals in their flocks, decided to obey and *"each one turned from his evil way and from the violence that was in his hands"* (Jon **3:8**). *"And the inhabitants of Nineveh believed God"* (Jon **3:5**), and when *"God saw their deeds, that they turned from their evil way; then God repented of the evil which he had said he would do unto them, and did not do it"* (Jon **3:10**).

This discourages Jonah because he wants to determine the results of the work to which God has called him. He wants Nineveh to be punished rather than spared, he judges the results of his own work harshly (Jon **4:5**), and he misses the joy of others. Do we do the same? When we lament the apparent lack of meaning and success in our work, do we forget that only God can see the true value of our labor?

It is possible that Jonah's hardness of heart was motivated by concern for his reputation. He proclaimed God's word that *"Nineveh will be thrown down to the earth"* (Jon **3:4**), but in the end it did not happen. Even if it was his own message that led the people of Nineveh to repent and avoid destruction, is it possible that Jonah felt that his credibility had been damaged? This idea seems to be at the heart of his complaint in Jonah **4:2**. He proclaimed what God told him to proclaim, but God changed his mind and made Jonah look like a fool. God is willing to *"repent of the evil he threatens"*, but Jonah is not willing to look like a fool, even if it means sparing the lives of **128,000** people. Like Jonah, it's good to ask ourselves if our attitudes and actions at work are more about making ourselves look good than bringing God's grace and love to those around us.

Yet even Jonah's small, hesitant moments of obedience to God brought blessings to those around him. On the boat, he confesses, *"I fear the Lord, the God of heaven"* (Jon **1:9**) and sacrifices himself for the sake of the people traveling with him. As a result, they are saved from the storm and also become followers of the Lord. *"And these men feared the Lord very much, and offered sacrifices to the Lord, and made vows to him"* (Jn **1:16**).

If we find that our work in God's service is curtailed by disobedience, resentment, laxity, fear, selfishness, or other infirmities, Jonah's experience can be an encouragement to us. Here we have a prophet who may have been even worse at faithful service than we are, but God accomplishes the fullness of His mission through Jonah's faltering, flawed, and intermittent service. By God's power, our flawed service can accomplish all that He plans.

God Cares for Those Who Answer His Call (Jonah 1:3, 12-14, 17; 2:10; 4:3-8)

———

Given Jonah's experience, we might fear that God's call will lead to disaster and hardship. Wouldn't it be easier to hope that God won't call us? It is true that responding to God's call may require great sacrifice and hardship. In the case of Jonah, however, the hardship does not come from God's call, but from Jonah's disobedience. The shipwreck and three days at sea inside the great fish are the direct result of his attempt to flee from God's presence. Later, his exposure to the sun and wind and his despair to the point of suicide (Jon **4:3-8**) are not God-ordained hardships, but are caused by Jonah's refusal to accept the blessings of a "*gracious and compassionate God, slow to anger and rich in mercy*" who is willing to repent of the evil he threatens (Jon **4:2**).

The truth is that God is always at work to care for and comfort Jonah. He causes people to have compassion on Jonah, as when the sailors try to row to dry land before accepting Jonah's offer to be thrown overboard (Jon **1:12-14**). God sends a fish to save Jonah from drowning (Jon **1:17**) and then commands it to throw Jonah to dry land (Jon **2:10**). He also allows Jonah to find favor among the hostile people of Nineveh, where they treat him with appreciation and pay attention to his message. In Jonah's time of greatest need, God provides him with shade and shelter in Nineveh (Jon **4:5-6**).

The case of Jonah is an example of how God's call to serve others in the workplace does not necessarily come at the expense of our own well-being. When we believe this, we remain trapped in a zero-sum game mentality. If God did extraordinary things to provide for Jonah even though he rejected the Lord's call, imagine the blessings he would have received if he had accepted the call from the beginning. The means to travel, friends willing to risk their lives for him, harmony with the natural world, shade and shelter, appreciation from the people he worked with, and amazing success in his work-imagine how great these blessings would have been if Jonah had accepted them as God intended. Even in the reduced form in which Jonah receives them, they show that God's call to service is also an invitation to blessing.

Conclusions to the Book of the Twelve Prophets

The books of the twelve prophets provide a unified perspective of the work at different times and situations in the life of Israel. In each case, they show that God is at work in the world and is willing to give the best to His people if they keep His covenant. Before the exile, the prophets admonished Israel's elites about their exercise of power and their faithfulness in worship. Their constant theme is that God only accepts worship that is accompanied by economic and political justice, because for Him there is no separation between the work of worship and the work of daily life. He does not accept that some prosper without contributing to the common good and to the poorest and most vulnerable members of society.

Israel's failure to do the work and worship that God demands leads to national disaster and exile in Babylon. During the exile, the prophets call the people to face their failures and discover that they had the opportunity to be faithful even in the worst of times. Again, their faithfulness is reflected in both their work and their worship. Those who work for selfish interests are no better than those who worship idols. Indeed, when work and the wealth that comes from it become ends in themselves, work is idolatry. But those who work righteously, in accordance with the covenant with God, will find that even in the worst circumstances, God is present in their work, bringing joy and fruit.

After the return from exile, the prophets exhort Israel to maintain godly priorities as they reestablish themselves in the land and rebuild it from the devastation. Again, economic development, fair trade, a government that provides for the common good, and work in service to others form the basis of true worship. All are called to work with God and the community of faith in pursuit of the peace and well-being that God desires for his creation.

This is our calling today, as it was for the ancient people of Israel. In the Hebrew order of the Old Testament, which is the same as the Christian order, the books of the Twelve Prophets provide the last words before the beginning of the New Testament. They therefore point to Jesus, who came to fulfill the prophets' longing for an abundant life in all areas of human activity, including work, thus fulfilling God's promise to Zechariah: "*The Lord of the heavenly hosts says, (Again the cities of Israel will be overflowing with prosperity)*" (Zech **1:17** NTV).

Don't miss out!

Visit the website below and you can sign up to receive emails whenever Bible Sermons publishes a new book. There's no charge and no obligation.

https://books2read.com/r/B-A-MZBS-AFRMC

Connecting independent readers to independent writers.

Did you love *Analyzing Labor Education in the 12 Prophets of the Bible*? Then you should read *Analyzing Labor Education in the Prophetic Books of the Bible*[1] by Bible Sermons!

2

Discover the transformative power of labor education in the prophetic books of the Bible. In this fascinating book, we will explore practical teachings that we can apply to our day from a historical biblical context. Through captivating stories and powerful biblical quotes, you will discover key principles for professional success and the practical skills needed to excel in any work environment. You will learn how to maintain integrity in the midst of pressure, make wise and ethical decisions, and

1. https://books2read.com/u/3LjPn7

2. https://books2read.com/u/3LjPn7

find your purpose and passion in your work. We will learn how to maintain our integrity and positive influence in a challenging corporate environment. In addition, we will discover practical tips for developing our professional skills, managing stress, and finding satisfaction in our daily work.This is not just another book on education or professional development; it is a comprehensive guide based on sound principles drawn from the prophetic books of the Bible. If you are looking for a new perspective for your work life and desire to grow both personally and professionally from a solid and timeless foundation such as God's Word, this book is for you.*Get ready to be empowered by these practical teachings! Discover how you can succeed in your career while living according to God's purpose!*

Also by Bible Sermons

A Collection of Biblical Sermons
The Power of Great Gospel Words
The Power of Prayer: Men Ought Always to Pray
The Power of the Single Life in Christ
Analyzing The Power of a Life in Christ

Bible Characters Collection
Analyzing Biblical Scenes: 62 Inspiring Christian Teachings
from the Old Testament

Notes in the New Testament
Analyzing Notes in the Book of Matthew: Fulfillments of Old
Testament Prophecies
Analyzing Notes in the Book of Mark: Finding Peace in
Difficult Times
Analyzing Notes in the Book of Luke: The Divine Love of Jesus
Revealed

Analyzing Notes in the Book of John: John's Contribution to the New Testament Scriptures
Analyzing Notes in the Book of the Acts of the Apostles: A Journey of Continuation in the Work of Jesus

Overflying The Bible
Symbols in the Bible: Healthy Christian Doctrine
Bible Introduction: Overflying The Bible from Genesis by Brethren in the Faith
Chronological Prophecy: Things That Will Happen on Earth
Bible Study: Genesis 1. Creation in Six Days

Teaching in the Bible Classroom
Studying Teaching in the Bible Classroom: A Teacher's Guide

The Education of Labor in the Bible
Analyzing the Education of Labor in Genesis: The Purpose of Life on Earth
Analyzing the Teaching of Labor in Exodus: From Slavery to Liberation
Analyzing the Labor Education in Leviticus: The Spirit of the Law at Work
Analyzing the Labor Education in Numbers: Israel's Desert Experience for Today's Challenges
Analyzing the Labor Education in Deuteronomy: A Perspective on Working Life Today

Analyzing Labor Education in the Pentateuch and Books
Historical
God's Guide for Work: Discovering God's Will for a Particular
Job
Analyzing Labor Education in Poetic Books
Analyzing Labor Education in the Prophetic Books of the Bible
Analyzing Labor Education in the 12 Prophets of the Bible

Standalone
Analyzing Notes in the 4 Gospels: Commentary Biblical
Analyzing What is to Come: God's Prophecies

About the Author

This bible study series is perfect for Christians of any level, from children to youth to adults. It provides an engaging and interactive way to learn the Bible, with activities and discussion topics that will help deepen your understanding of scripture and strengthen your faith. Whether you're a beginner or an experienced Christian, this series will help you grow in your knowledge of the Bible and strengthen your relationship with God. Led by brothers with exemplary testimonies and extensive knowledge of scripture, who congregate in the name of the Lord Jesus Christ throughout the world.